HITMAN-
BAKER-
CASKETMAKER

Other Books of Poetry by Klecko

Out for a Lark
The Bluebeard of Happiness
A Pox Upon Your Blessings
Houdini in St. Paul
My British Hindu Bible
Robert Bly and The Monk in His Cell
Mayor 4 Life
Brando Land

HITMAN-
BAKER-
CASKETMAKER

Aftermath of an American's Clash with ICE

by Klecko

PARIS MORNING
PUBLICATIONS

Published in 2019 by Paris Morning Publications
www.parismorningpublications.com

Published and printed in the United States of America
ISBN: 978-0-578-42629-7

Cover design by Audrey Campbell
www.ataudrey.com

This book is dedicated to the Home Ec teachers of District #281 in gratitude for their training, love and support.

EPILOGUE

Mexicans in the Parking Lot

ON THE MORNING OF MY 55TH BIRTHDAY

Mother and I sat in a café
She asked what I was ordering
She asked about my new job
How things were going in general
I confessed
It occurred to me recently
I was probably alcoholic
But a functional alcoholic
Destroying my life wasn't my primary concern
I was curious, why numb felt best
Mother smiled and explained
Drink up kiddo, you don't need to worry
Since you were small
I've always known you were a mystic
The whiskey will fade without effort
Because now you've reached an age
Where your journey is going to make sense
You won't need to feel numb any longer
The bill was paid, and as we went our separate ways
I wondered if what Mother said was true
After a moment, it occurred to me
I couldn't remember an instance
When her instinct wasn't spot-on

UNDER AN ALMOST SUPER MOON

As usual
We shared indifference, we shared darkness
From opposite ends of a park bench
Like God damn gargoyles with nothing left to defend
Distracted by classifieds
My comic book posed the question
Do you know how to pick up chicks?
I didn't, so I was intrigued
Grandma slid over and hung over my shoulder
Reading my mind
And lighting the evening's final cigarette, she offered advice
Don't forget, you're a Polack, and not very smart
Which means you'll have to work twice as hard
If you want to land a good woman
And then she stared into the distance
With a look a boy couldn't be expected to understand
Until years later, when his heart became broken
So maybe
Maybe my mean grandmother was a blessing
Especially when she reminded me
I'm a Polack and not very smart
But at least I am easy on the eyes
Because I look just like her

MY FIRST TOOL BOX

One might suggest it was the result
Of growing up without a father
Others have offered
It's merely genetic disposition
Either way, I've come to terms with it
I lack mechanical aptitude
I'll never forget the time my grandfather
Stopped by my apartment
How his eyes sparkled when he spotted
My Craftsman toolbox on the kitchen table
He opened it without permission
But just as the examination started
His enthusiasm waned
When he noticed the contents were
Fondant molds and pastry tips
Though the moment was awkward
I remained secure in my masculinity
But when he picked up my textbook
Wilton's Course in Flowers and Cake Design
What I wouldn't have given
To have an ample place to hide

WHAT CHEF JOAN IDA TOLD ME

I thought of you recently
When I was in Rome
Gathering inspiration for a new menu
I was in my hotel room
Feeling kind of lonely
Then I heard a loud noise overhead
It sounded as if something
Was about to land on the roof
I became curious and peeked through the curtains
To my surprise, I saw the Pope
Riding shotgun in a helicopter
And when he noticed me, he waved
Later I was told
These flights are not uncommon
He enjoys praying for the Holy City from above
The whole event was so startling
Did I mention I waved back?
As he flew away
I wished you could have been there

REPUBLICAN NATIONAL CONVENTION

When the RNC came to the Capital City
Municipal workers constructed a holding pen
A huge cage attached to the police station
Just outside the window of our bakery
Over the course of a week
Lunchtime was met with anticipation
The bakers born in St. Paul constructed crude banners
Offering encouragement to howling protesters pent up
While the Mexican-born bakers asked among themselves
What is there to protest
When you get to live in America

FACTORY TOWN

Production takes place in the part of the city
Where beauty will take no root
Cinder-block borders create sanctuary
For those who prefer not to get noticed
Yet, there she sits
Alone in the break room
Next to the Coke machine
And it's that very moment
His fortune whispers
This is the place to be

124 DEGREES

With two hours before sunrise
The last baker enters the break room
Joining a crew, soaked and faded
Their shift hasn't started
Condensation on windows
And Gatorade puddles
Serve as warnings
This won't be a day for talking
In silence, they wait
Listening to the compressors
Wheezing for air on the other side
Of the oven room door
Each considers leaving
But fears being the first
To turn tail
While their brothers face the dragon
Only years later will they realize
Why they had to carry on
It wasn't for themselves
But each other

TROPHIES OF CONQUEST

Knowing how much I dislike Garrison Keillor
Without provocation
The pastry chef entered my office smirking
Because she had received
A second-hand invite to a gala
Taking place at his home
That very night
Steal the bastard's salt and pepper shakers
We'll put them in the break room
My request offered no purpose
Yet the pastry chef called it genius
The following morning
As I prepared to hear a detailed account
The pastry chef simply yawned
While handing me a package with contents
I'm not at liberty to discuss

MEXICANS IN THE PARKING LOT

After 14 hours in front of an oven
Breeze feels good, beer tastes good
Both could be found outside in the parking lot
Where a dozen bakers circled a cooler
Drinking beer quietly, starting without me
Most of them were half my age
All of them were Mexican
The youngest handed me a Modelo
I opened the can, tilted it and swallowed
Noticing the satisfaction of the crew
As they faced the breeze to receive a reward
That would only pay dividends
Until the cooler was empty

DUSTY'S BAR AND DAGOS

The red carpet would be rolled out if I said yes and crossed the river
To join Scott Vetsch and his ruffians at Dusty's Bar and Dagos
I accepted, and as I left the Capital City
By way of the 94 & Dale on-ramp
A homeless guy stood on the median and begged for change
He extended his arms, he only had one hand, and a stump
I gave him nothing and drove away
Exiting 94, on the West Broadway off-ramp
A homeless guy stood on the median and begged for change
Swear to God, he also had one hand and a stump
I blurted out "FUCK ME" as I gave him nothing and drove away
At Dusty's I waited for Scott to buy me a drink
He didn't, so I went to the bar and ordered
When I turned around the opening act started
He had both of his hands
But they were attached to his elbows instead of his wrists
I was alarmed and sat down
Wondering what the Goddess was trying to reveal
Was what I was witnessing simply genetic coincidence
Or a sign that I should start a new religion
As I considered this
I remembered I didn't have the patience for spirituality
But it seemed like a shame to waste this mojo
So on the way home I stopped and bought lottery tickets

CONVERSATION WITH A
SUPER AMERICA CASHIER

She had to be 50 years old
50 pounds overweight
Her eyes seem drained as she leaned against the counter
Telling me her complications related to diabetes
As I waited for her to ring up my order
She interrupted her rant to remind me
The Powerball payout was at an obscene amount
Then she told me it was against the law to say this
But she had a hunch she was going to pull the winner
In addition to my Diet Coke and 5-Hour Energy shots
I bought a Powerball ticket and slid it across the counter
And asked where she would go after she won
Her face went blank, until she explained
I have no idea where a person should go
I've only been here
And Nebraska

BIRTHDAYS WITH A FIRST WIFE

I still see her lips moving in slow motion
Forming promises of love
But I have to believe she was uncertain of her feelings
Since once a year, for consecutive years
I was given birthday treats
Purchased at the grocery
Or perhaps a high-end gas station
When I flipped the lid open and stared into the box
The cupcakes were always frosted
Chocolate or vanilla
Candy confetti exploded in rainbow colors
Sweet pieces of shrapnel scattered across the parchment
But the part I remember most
Is those scary plastic clown heads
Periscoping through the frosting
Smiling at my discomfort

WEDDING CAKE TRANSPORT

More often than not, I find it bad form
To call a Metro Mobility driver a fucking tool
But when they change lanes without using their blinker
They do so without considering
A bride's heart is constructed to make allowances
To adapt to deformity
As long as it's contained within the flesh
But, in the event the village baker arrives
Handing off a cake with even the slightest blemish
There will be no consideration
For climate, road construction
Or a fleeting loss of dexterity
When a nitroglycerin delivery gets bungled
The result is nothing more than a momentary KABOOM
But God help the baker who botches a wedding cake delivery
Because he will be trapped in an eternal memory
Filled with contempt

A PREFERENCE OF LEMON

Mary Beth had pictures of her uncle
Eugene McCarthy on the wall
Postcards of her ex-husband Peter
Of Peter, Paul and Mary
Standing next to the Dalai Lama
Whiskey moguls, hotel tycoons, a state senator
And an attorney general, standing, circling
Surrounding a cake that I brought to commemorate
The 80th birthday of Capital City's Poet Laureate
The Duchess
On the day proceeding this day, Mary Beth called
And commissioned me to write a poem for the event
After answering yes, but before signing off
It was mentioned in passing
If I had any extra cake at the bakery
Cake that wasn't chocolate
I was welcome to bring that, too
I took the hint and took my time
Baking and wondering
What would be appropriate
What would be my message
For an 80-year-old Poet Laureate and her tribe
I decided to tell the truth

SINGLE GLOW

Due to champagne and festive atmosphere
The program fell behind, I waited for my cue
A man with a delicate bracelet beseeched the caterer
To repeat the story he told in the pantry
The caterer obliged by stating that Peter
From Peter, Paul and Mary just got back from Japan
Where he toured with the Dalai Lama
Singing songs he wrote to combat bullies
Due to champagne and festive atmosphere
I waited, and wondered
If I had moderated the night Dylan went electric
Or performed in D.C. at Dr. King's civil rights march
Would I need to sing anti-bullying songs to remain relevant
I wasn't judging, just uncertain
But certain in the fact that life changes when you get old
At last, my name was called
I led a chorus of "Happy Birthday"
And after Duchess blew out the candle
The room became silent
All eyes fell upon me
As my poem was about to begin
In 3 - 2 - 1 . . .

GIRL CAKE

Nobody understands
The thought process of women
On the anniversary of their birth
Quite like the village baker
For he has set 1000 cakes
Before the fairer species
And he has deduced
What the majority will miss
That women aren't thinking about
The arc of their life
The losses they have suffered
Or how many candles are blazing
She simply wants dessert

MEXICANS IN THE PARKING LOT

After 14 hours in front of an oven
Breeze feels good, beer tastes good
Both could be found outside in the parking lot
Where a dozen bakers circled a cooler
Drinking beer quietly, starting without me
Most of them were half my age
All of them were Mexican
The youngest handed me a Modelo
I opened the can, tilted it and swallowed
Noticing the satisfaction of the crew
As they faced the breeze to receive a reward
That would only pay dividends
Until the cooler was empty

THINKING OF TEXAS

Office door closed, eyes wide open
I leaned back, watching minuscule particles of flour
Hanging underneath a fluorescent light
Amidst the glow, amidst a haze
I think I was thinking about Texas when I turned
And saw the Poet Finley's post on my monitor
It said
A Buddhist chaplain stopped by this morning
To announce my daughter died last night
I became dizzy
The silence increased
She worked for me at the bakery
When I broke the news to her supervisor
A former Pentecostal minister, he explained
The family is traumatized
There is nothing we can do
Except see to their comfort
Then he made out a list
And encouraged me to act immediately

ITEMS TO BRING A FAMILY IN CRISIS

Water
Groceries
Paper Plates
Solo Cups
Plastic Cutlery
Paper Towels
Toilet Paper
Toothpaste
Tide
Magazines
Chocolate

AN AUGUST MORNING

After parking my truck, I paused
Not knowing how to proceed
The chain link fence was mangled, the lawn overgrown
An appropriate place to launch a young life
Not end it
As I stood in the street, two men joined me
One flew in from Paris
The other from San Francisco
After minimal banter, we climbed a staircase
And examined an apartment, hotter than a sauna
Hours passed, we scrubbed, packed and hauled
A lifetime of possessions to dumpsters and storage
None of us seemed able to find words of importance
The best we could muster was brief eye contact
And soft smiles
When the task was complete, and it was time to leave
An awkward moment presented itself
Maybe we were traumatized
Because we didn't know how to disperse
There was nothing obvious to state
So we climbed into our vehicles
And drove away realizing
Some moments were best ended without ceremony

THE UNIVERSITY CLUB SVENGALI

The Poet Finley stood irreverent
Bypassing the podium
Insensitive to protocol
Replacing verse
With an account of loss
The stage became a confessional
Of which he took full advantage
By starting off the evening
Announcing he fired God
He didn't qualify as an agnostic
He didn't convert to atheism
He fully believed in a supreme being
And terminated this companion
In ceremony and silence
Half the audience became unnerved
Pointing out that heresy starts
The moment belief stops
But the rest of us fell into a trance
Knowing what our dear friend had lost

TAVERN ON GRAND

The man said something about Kentucky
The women mentioned she was adopted in Korea
They sat across from one another
With distance and postures
That made it difficult to determine their relationship
Korea pulled out a pack of cigarettes
And said she needed to step outside
Even though she probably shouldn't
Because one of her lungs filled with blebs and collapsed
Twice
Kentucky returned a look of disbelief
Before confessing one of his lungs collapsed
Twice
After the second surgery
The surgeons scraped the blebs in such a manner
That they were encouraged to adhere to the rib cage
Everything would be ok
As long as he didn't break any ribs
Korea pulled out a lighter, Kentucky followed suit
Both exiting toward a parking lot
With cigarettes dangling from their mouths
And a certainty that on this night
They'd escape their probable outcome

TAVERN ON GRAND

Amidst the crowd, I sat alone, comfortable at the bar
Wondering if I would fare well as a Trappist monk
After several drinks, I decided to take a vow of silence
If only for the night
When my tumbler was empty, and the barkeep approached
I simply pointed to the Jameson and that was enough
To create a perfect balance between white noise and whiskey
To my left sat a woman in a booth
Fidgeting with a handful of coins, a quarter escaped her grasp
And rolled circle patterns across the floor
Until it hit my clog and lay motionless
I didn't retrieve or return the coin
Because I was feeling a sense of monastic entitlement
To my surprise, the woman got down on all fours
And crawled toward my stool, her face hovered over my feet
Her position unnerved me enough that I broke my vow
By asking if a quarter was really worth groveling over
The woman stood, snapped and informed me
Not all of us have money to burn
Befuddled, I ordered another drink
Embarrassed I didn't have a clue
How limited my monastic skill set was

TAVERN ON GRAND

She was tall, shapely, had high cheekbones
He was squatty with a pockmarked face
She was beautiful, he wasn't
I caught a glimpse of them working together
Preparing walleye tacos, side by side
Every time the service door swung open
I caught her smiling
Her eyes told the truth
She was enamored
I wondered how it transpired
What could such a perfect specimen
See in a blemished cook
Then it occurred to me
Hairnets were the common denominator
Both of them wore polypropylene bouffant caps
The ones that look like toilet seat covers
The ones that strip you of dignity
The moment you slide it on your skull
Then it occurred to me
Hairnets force us to look past vanity
And into the heart
KABOOM, I finally cracked the code
Once I realized
Love would be easier to obtain
If hairnets were passed out across the globe
And all of us were brave enough to conform

MEXICANS IN THE PARKING LOT

After 14 hours in front of an oven
Breeze feels good, beer tastes good
Both could be found outside, in the parking lot
Where a dozen bakers circled a cooler
Drinking beer quietly, starting without me
Most of them were half my age
All of them were Mexican
The youngest handed me a Modelo
I opened the can, tilted it and swallowed
Noticing the satisfaction of the crew
As they faced the breeze to receive a reward
That would only pay dividends
Until the cooler was empty

THE SUPER BOWL

During the bakery's most profitable year
The Twin Cities was going to host their second Super Bowl
Life had never been better
Our bakery was honored to have the bread contracts
The Vikings were still in contention
Most of us liked our team's chance
The spotlight was bright
Media swarmed
Pointing cameras on a city of people who dared to dream
I, on the other hand, wouldn't be able to watch the game
Or bake for it
I had been selected by a French panel
To spend Super Bowl Sunday attending their baking expo in Paris
It was mentioned with emphasis
That I was the only American invited
Life had never been better

THE AUDIT

16 days before the Super Bowl
The results of what was thought to be
A routine immigration audit arrived
Indicating 23 employees had invalid I-9s
Most of the 23 were supervisors
Most of the 23 had worked with me for decades
A lawyer was called, took note and predicted
ICE agents wouldn't offer flexibility
And even if they did, your staff will bolt
The moment you inform them of their status
I mentioned, I thought the crew would stick
The lawyer didn't respond
The silence exploded
And I heard KABOOM
For the first time, in a long time
I wasn't sure what to do, so I went home
To a space where sleep was replaced by tears
And episodes of Shark Tank

RALLY OF DESPAIR

Never before had the crew been called
To assemble for a mandatory meeting
They stared, I spoke
The results of our I-9 audit arrived
Half of you aren't qualified for employment
The lawyer said you can work 10 more days
But he assured me you wouldn't
He said you'd be afraid and bolt
If that's true, I wouldn't blame you
But I propose we tell our accounts
We are closing after Friday's bake
Our purpose has been taken
But not our dignity, I suggest we use it
Before moving on
Before plugging into a new normal
The packing supervisor responded
You can't close the doors
It's our fault, we will work for free
Until you find replacements
I smiled and said no, not without you
And the crew went back to work

KARMA MATTERS

Don't hope for luck, make your own
Was the mantra of the Vikings organization
That's why they invited Millie Wall
A 99-year-old woman, soon to be 100
Who watched every Vikings game
Sitting in her living room
With a cocktail in one hand
And a foam brick in the other
That she threw at her TV
Every time the Vikings faltered
The media ran with the story
Minnesota loved her
On game day, she arrived in a limo
A red carpet was rolled out
Don't hope for luck, make your own
On the final play of the game
The Vikings completed a 61-yard pass
For a touchdown and the right
To advance to the conference finals
Millie was delighted, but not surprised
By the Minnesota miracle

KARMA MATTERS

On the evening of the NFC Championship
An hour before kickoff, breaking news reported
Eagles fans were booing, spitting
And throwing full cans of beer
At Vikings fans who traveled to support their team
I'd heard Eagles fans were a tough lot
I'd heard they once threw snowballs at Santa Claus
But when I found out young men in South Philly
Paraded the streets waving banners announcing
Fuck Millie
I began to relax knowing
You can't talk shit about a state's adopted grandmother
Without paying a price
Without pissing off karma
It was that moment I realized
Tonight's contest was academic
Karma couldn't unfold in any pattern
That didn't allow the Vikings
To play at home during the Super Bowl

MEDIA JACKALS

The Vikings lost, the city was numb
The media needed a story
They stirred until they found their morsel
Klecko Fumbles During Super Bowl
City Scrambles For Bread
Media jackals barraged the bakery
Circling the wounded, looking for quotes
Because I wanted to pay my employees
Because I wanted to pay my purveyors
I had to comment—no comment
The moment I made our demise official
ICE would level fines
A reporter from WCCO-TV entered our office
After receiving a no comment response
She lied by reporting that five supervisors fled
Because they were afraid of ICE
Days later City Pages reported the same
Underneath a photoshopped picture
Of ICE raiding a building
That was meant to depict our bakery
They compromised our dignity for headlines
Insinuating we were cowards
Knowing we were helpless
And in no position to defend ourselves

LUNCH WITH OSO

Every day
For 21 years, I ate lunch with Oso
The morning bread mixer
In the employee break room
Where we combined our food
Onto a single plate
On the final day of production
After setting out our meal
Neither one of us ate
We weren't hungry
Neither one of us could sleep
We were past tired
It had been a 90-hour work week
So we just sat together quietly
I didn't know what to say
So I asked
You gonna be ok?
He nodded yes before explaining
The biggest mistake I made
Was I got too comfortable
As a Mexican
I should have known better

THE LAST NIGHT OF PRODUCTION

All week long I worried
About the final moment
About saying goodbye
I was afraid I would cry
But I didn't take into consideration
How deluded emotions can get
After spending 18 hours
In front of an oven
When the last loaf was pulled
Everyone was beyond exhaustion
Nobody hugged
Or marked the moment with ceremony
We were numb
But in our numbness
Fear and sorrow couldn't touch us
And because of this
Our legacy didn't cease
It evaporated

AFTERMATH

On Super Bowl Sunday
I returned to the bakery
To liquidate equipment
Alone in the oven room
I stood in emptiness
Silence
Not even a ghost lingered
Our pulse was gone
I didn't like the loneliness
So I turned on the radio
It was reported
Millie Wall was skipping the Super Bowl
Because she had pneumonia
I didn't believe a word of it
During the last few weeks
I had become old enough to understand
Attending the party is meaningless
When you're not accompanied by your tribe

MEXICANS IN THE PARKING LOT

DRINKING TEA IN TED KING'S GARDEN

In the time it took Ted to roll a cigarette
He told me about the beat poets
How they didn't have a scene
Because scenes are created by imitators
He also pointed out
If I'm ever going to make it as a method poet
I need to write for the stage
Not for the page
He also suggested I stop reading poetry
And start going to art shows
Or dance recitals
But most importantly, Ted told me to be honest
Audiences aren't used to that
And it's always in a poet's best interest
To keep an audience off-balance
Then he asked
If I had ever been to San Francisco
I said no
He smiled, then explained
The light there is beautiful
Different than anywhere else
You need to go there

INTERNATIONAL ORANGE

After she goes to sleep
After a couple of chapters, after a couple of drinks
I reach numb, and that's when it occurs to me
She deserves to hear me say
How wonderful she is
But in the morning, I leave before she wakes
And when I return, the world is bright
And I am no longer numb
Last summer I made her smile
By taking her to New York City
So we could hold hands
And walk across the Brooklyn Bridge
This year, my inability to communicate continued
So I took her to San Francisco
To experience the Golden Gate Bridge
Halfway across, she leaned against the guardrail
To watch the fog consume Alcatraz
When it disappeared, she smiled
And told me I was good to her
But I knew better
She deserved more

SUNDAY AT THE SFMOMA

I seldom find people taller than me
Standing next to me in art galleries
But on this occasion, I did
The room was empty except for me and him
He had to be half my age
Bangs scraped his chin
His T-shirt said FLIP
The kid asked if I liked Diebenkorn
I told him I came from Minnesota to find out
Because Jimmy the artist told me
He used color better than any American painter
FLIP asked if I wanted to sit on the bench
Across from his favorite painting
Cityscape #1
I nodded, we sat, we stared
Neither one of us said a word
After a half hour, FLIP squeezed my hand
With a level of pressure that suggested
He enjoyed our moment
Then he got up and walked out
Usually I don't like being touched by strangers
But on this occasion I did

PIER 39

Because it became her new routine
I drank espresso and sat patiently
While she stared at sea lions
Scrounging for kelp
Acting like monkeys, entertaining tourists
Most stayed briefly
But we spent hours, because
It's hard to tell when she's happy
She doesn't smile often
But she smiled here
More than she does back home
When I take her to see monkeys

CITY LIGHTS BOOKSTORE

After eating pasta, I popped in
Hoping I might catch Ferlinghetti
He wasn't there
I strolled ground level
Becoming disappointed
The store seemed nice, but not legendary
Until I saw a staircase, and climbed it
Up top was a room filled with people
Reading poetry
If wardrobe served as an indicator
These customers were mechanics and nurses
Not MFA writers
I felt happy and jealous, I picked up a copy
Of Wislawa Szymborska's collected poems
A guy in flannel noticed and asked
If I had been to Poland
I said no, have you
He said no, but he'd been to Amsterdam
I asked if he made it to the Anne Frank house
He said yes, but he got stoned before entering
And it was too much, he had to leave
Then he advised me not to get stoned if I went
I told him
I'd keep that in mind

VERTIGO

The very moment we entered the Muir Woods
I remembered the scene with Jimmy Stewart
And Kim Novak, how they held odd postures
Surrounded by silence and sequoias
Engaged in disturbing conversation
Alone, disconnected, in a space so remote
Even God couldn't find them
My hope was we could have that intimacy
But the deeper we went in
The louder things got
Children in wheelchairs, howling
Old women speed-walking
In Spandex and shawls
The lout from Tennessee
Explaining to Japanese visitors
Where to find the best hamburgers in America
I looked at you, and smiled at my stupidity
Wondering what possessed me to think
That we could have the forest to ourselves
But that's how I'd always envisioned our moment
Who would have guessed
Our script would be
More complicated than Hitchcock's

ON MY WAY TO ALCATRAZ

For the longest time, we stood on deck
Waiting for the ferry to take us
To gawk at a former generation's hell
Seated close by, at the end of a bench
A family of four, everyone but mom
Dressed in Belgium soccer kits
When the boat pulled out
The smallest Belgian, a boy
Bent over and vomited on the deck
After most of the content was expelled
Mom popped up, hugged the boy tight
Placing him in her lap
Moments passed, then moments more
The Belgians moved past the moment
Without contacting the crew
To clean up the deck
To rinse the kid's mouth
Their eyes were fixed forward
As we bobbed up and down
My phone rang
It was a reporter from MPR
Wondering if I was willing to talk yet

MY SOCIAL MEDIA RESPONSE
TO MY MPR INTERVIEW

I almost never talk about politics on social media
But today I am going to make an exception
Below is the first time I spoke out
About what happened at St. Agnes Baking Co.
Although this story has some truth
It doesn't contain many of the quotes
I felt were more relevant
To a difficult topic

MY SOCIAL MEDIA RESPONSE
TO MY MPR INTERVIEW

I don't think the issue is illegals working abroad
Politicians have had forever to remedy this
The truth is first-world nations
Are using illegal work forces to bolster their economy
It's going on all over the world
The sad thing about this is that the illegals
Bust ass to bring your life value and luxury
Plain and simple, most buildings in your neighborhood
Are filled with cleaners, cooks, and general laborers
These people provide benefits to you
While living in abject fear
I don't like standing on soap boxes
It seldom makes impact
But just for today
I am announcing to my community and government
I stand by Mexicans
And all people who work hard for a better life

CLOSING THOUGHTS

Truth be told
I'll never get over it
Millions of dollars, millions of loaves
Vanished in a single Super Bowl run
Because my crew wasn't in compliance
With the laws of the land
That's on me, I'll accept the scorn
And even the criticism
But I'll never apologize
Because for a quarter of a century
We fed the Twin Cities
With the best bread known to Minnesota
My only regret is
I cannot list the names
Of the bakers who worked
Late nights, holidays and weekends
To ensure you received
Loaves to build tradition on
According to some
Those services are criminal

AN ENCORE OF FEATHERS

After dismantling hummingbird feeders
Mother escorted me to the winter feeding station
To assemble a heated birdbath
Frost on our breath, frost on the lawn
Two crows were ground feeding, I wished I'd worn mittens
I mentioned this hobby was nice, but maybe out of balance
Relatives had reported a prolonged absence
Mother smiled, pointing up toward a telephone wire
Those mourning doves weren't here last year
Now they stop by every day and splash around like crazy
Nothing is predictable in my backyard
I've learned to be comfortable alone
I prefer to be alone
I love being with the birds
They seem to be on a higher level
St. Francis understood this, and you would, too
If you took time to study the saints
Then she kissed me and went inside
Leaving me to watch nuthatches and chickadees
Nuthatches eat upside down
And I would have liked to watch them longer
But I didn't have my mittens and went inside
Realizing Mother wasn't wrong

Intermission

PREQUEL

Hitman-Baker-Casketmaker

CRONKITE CRIED

On a Friday, in Inglewood, California
Mother stood over the ironing board
Folding sheets and pillow cases
Watching . . . *As the World Turns*
Doing her best to disregard doubt
She needed a job because she needed a divorce
And wasn't it ironic
That her doctor introduced her to a new invention
Called birth control pills, 12 weeks after I was born
Her lineage was Polish, her tribe withheld emotion
And even though she was about to embark on an escape
Without benefit of resources
She remained true to the code, never shedding a tear
Until the regular featured broadcast was interrupted
By a bulletin announcing
President Kennedy had been shot
Cronkite cried, which seemed to give permission
For my mother to open the floodgates
And she cried throughout the night
Knowing once we left
There would be no turning back
And thus, our journey began

AN ERA

During an era when divorce was uncommon
Much of my custody was spent in the presence
Of a grandfather who mentored with reluctance
When you're not wanted, tolerance will do
During our better moments, he'd escort me into his office
Open the safe and pull out plastic bags
Filled with newspaper clippings and mementoes
Featuring Mantle, Mays and Billy Martin
There was also a Babe Ruth magazine
I wasn't allowed to touch it
It became apparent to all parties concerned
There was no reason to believe
Our connection would diminish soon
This made the obvious apparent
If I didn't develop an appreciation for the Bronx Bombers
Life would become more miserable
Than it already was

AN INVENTORY OF MOTHER'S BOYFRIENDS

Some have suggested
Unraveling Mother's love life encroaches on irreverent
I disagree
Unraveling Mother's love life introduces me
To when innocence overlapped prime
As I list the inventory of Mother's boyfriends
You can't count the taxi driver I saw her kissing in the driveway
That was nothing more than straight sex I was informed
But when you move past lust, into matters of the heart
My mother once loved
A chopper pilot who was sent to Vietnam
We sent him packages until the jungle took him away
There was the black veterinarian who drove a gold Corvette
He had Playboy magazines scattered across his living room
Discovering them was better than finding buried treasure
There was a man who looked like Fabio
He sold me baseball cards at Tom Thumb
On their first date he gave me 20 packs of Topps
Guaranteeing one of them would contain
A Dave Winfield rookie card
But Mother dumped him because he was too young
And then the cadence of romance halted
Until the World Series
When she brought home Whiskey Willie

FIGHT OF THE CENTURY

My father only hung out with me once when I was a kid
It was a Monday, and he took me to the Metropolitan Sports Center
To watch the Ali / Frazier fight
This was way before cable television
I was one of only 17,000 people in Minnesota
That got to witness this historic event
The arena was filled with cigar smoke
And old men wearing plaid sports coats
I was the only child in attendance
Ali was the undefeated champion
But stripped of his title for refusing to enlist in the military
Frazier was the current champ
And had annihilated all his previous opponents
The entire planet waited to see who would win
When the fight was over, and most of the crowd had filed out
My father didn't want to leave, so the two of us sat there
Watching the cleaning crew prepare to start their shift
Finally, my dad looked up and confessed in an awkward voice
When you get older, you're going to realize I'm a shitty father
But I hope you will remember
That I had two tickets to the fight of the century
And I wanted to take you

THE 1972 OAKLAND A'S

Grandfather believed baseball wasn't America's pastime
The New York Yankees were, my generation disagreed
We felt the Yankees became sterile when Mickey Mantle retired
To our defense came an insurance salesman from Chicago
A rat who feasted on the eggs of dinosaurs
His name was Charlie Finley
He owned the Oakland A's
And believed baseball would become lucrative
If those in attendance had fun
He dressed his squad in day-glo uniforms
Comprised of citrus colors
His pitching staff had colorful nicknames
Rollie Fingers, Catfish Hunter, Vida Blue
And Blue Moon Odom
Charlie petitioned for orange baseballs, night games
And the designated hitter
Other owners wrote him off as a heretic
But to every boy born in the 60s
He was the man who saved baseball

THE 1972 WORLD SERIES

Mother resumed routine and ritual
Making stylish adjustments in front of her vanity
Preparing for another first date
The doorbell rang, I was instructed to answer
A man wearing a bomber jacket walked in
He shook my hand and introduced himself as Willie
I told him to follow me, the World Series was about to start
We stepped into my bedroom, the national anthem began
Willie insisted the Reds would sweep
Because Reggie Jackson was injured
Leaving Oakland without a long ball threat
I reminded him that pitching wins championships
And the A's bullpen would shut down Rose and Morgan
Willie smirked while informing me
That wasn't the way his bookie saw it
I asked him if he wanted to bet a dollar
As Mother stepped in announcing she was ready to go
Willie asked me to find him a beer
And told Mother the night wasn't going anywhere
So maybe they should watch an inning with the kid

BULLETPOINTS AND BACKSTORY
OF WHISKEY WILLIE

* Oldest of five siblings
* Grew up in an apartment over a bar called Barney's Funhouse
* Mother skated in the roller derby
* Father was a pool shark who hung in the same circle as Minnesota Fats
* Pathfinder in the United States Marine Corps
* Followed the Yankees and Lakers religiously
* Rode a Harley Davidson
* Owned a carpet installation service
* Kept whiskey in the bedroom
* Screamed in the middle of the night at ghosts he met in Korea
* Sought help from Alcoholics Anonymous and TV evangelists
* Adored my mother

TV WITH WILLIE

I won our game of foosball, and winners got to choose
After rifling through the channels, I selected *The Quiet Man*
The film was almost over
John Wayne was about to fight Maureen O'Hara's brother
I explained to Willie, this was the longest fight in Hollywood history
The two men exchanged blows
As they stumbled through fields, across the village, and into a river
Where a priest declared round one complete
John Wayne and Maureen O'Hara's brother took a break
Inside a pub, where drinks were on the house
Willie slouched in a position that suggested he was unimpressed
When I asked him what he thought, he offered
Most fights are over after one punch, good fighters are patient
They take their time and if they find a weakness, they exploit it
I thought about this as Willie left the room
When he returned with beer and licorice, I asked
Can someone be exploited when both sides are equal
Willie smiled and explained
If your opponent's flaw isn't obvious, that's when you walk away
It's never a good idea to put your body on the line
Unless you have a decisive advantage
Then he told me it was smart to discuss these things
Because that's what men do

CHRISTMAS EVE AT THE GOLDEN LEAF BAR

The horseshoe pit behind the bar was free of restrictions
A place where Willie could smoke weed
And I could drink whiskey, under age
Our actions had no attachment to rebellion
We were simply killing time, waiting until we could return home
To a place where Mother would remain unglued
Until the first holiday guest arrived and the party began
The horseshoe pit behind the bar was absent of order
A place where fights broke out
And participation was predicated by proximity
As was the case, on this day, on Christmas Eve
After a drug deal went bad, and the culprit in question
Tried to deflect guilt, by pointing to Willie and calling him a pussy
For wearing a brown leather jacket instead of black
The fight was over before it started
The bloodied culprit was dragged to the alley
Willie asked if I was frightened, I said no
Then he smiled and told me I should have been
Because fear is a good thing
And people who don't make friends with it
End up in dumpsters

HITMEN IN THE KITCHEN

About a month before I moved out of my parents' house
Two hitmen stood in our kitchen
They were high school friends of Willie
Visiting on a one-night layover
Wearing Italian suits that cost more than my car
When the whiskey bottle was empty
The ashtrays full
The contract killers hinted
It would be convenient to crash at our place
My mother answered, by not answering
The following morning, she entertained whimsy
By trying to imagine the daily routine of an assassin
Deducing that they probably took their meals at restaurants
Their love from pay dates
And you just had to figure, they had all their laundry sent out
I thought about it for a second, looking up from my cereal bowl
Replying, if I had to make people disappear for a living
I'd wash my own clothes to bring some normalcy to life
We both laughed
Until our eyes met
Then we became frightened

ORDERLY

From my experience, the most intimate experience
Takes place watching people die
I discovered this working third shift
On a security floor for criminals and the insane
Unstable residents too old
To remain in general population
I was hired for size and strength
And paid an hourly wage to exert
The required amount of patience it takes
To pacify fading souls
When old people are close to death, they seldom sleep at night
Fearing once they close their eyes, they'll never wake again
Tick-Tock, murmuring hallway voices
Tick-Tock, footsteps pounding linoleum
Tick-Tock, holding hands in the dark
Waiting for that final moment
When everything important and unimportant
Becomes jumbled enough for them to trust
That if they don't wake up
I will remember them

THE LODGE

It was sold as a vacation getaway
Fishing opener, with Willie and some friends
Our van stopped just short of Canada
In front of a dilapidated shack
Inside Willie introduced me to men
Who sat around a table, sampling from a Lazy Susan
That offered pills, powder and weed
On the counter were bottles
Whiskey and vodka, but mostly whiskey
To my surprise, there wasn't any beer
Within a short time the men dispersed
Into small groups and separated
By all indications, nobody was here to wet a line
As I began to consider the gathering's purpose
I poured myself a drink with the understanding
That my acceptance could only be purchased with silence
When Willie returned, he handed me forty dollars
To play poker with the men
As I stuck the cash in my pocket he told me
That I could try anything except the pills
But not to go overboard
Because the following morning
He wanted me to meet Tim

THE BOAT

In darkness, I woke to scattered sounds of men snoring
And the glowing cherry of a cigarette
Pulsing in rhythm, attached to a silhouette
That motioned me to follow outside
The smoker introduced himself as Tim
While heading to the dock
Where he told me to hop into the boat
And start rowing toward the center of the lake
When our destination was achieved, I was told to relax
For the first time it occurred to me
My obedience to this unknown circumstance
Was the result of nothing more than my faith in Willie
The sun had yet to rise, I felt mist on my face as Tim asked
If I had the nerve to make somebody disappear
I had a thousand questions, asked zero and answered yes
My decision ended the conversation
Floating, drifting, floating
Listening to the sound of waves slapping the boat
Until Tim pointed at a light and told me to row towards it
To a general store that would be open by the time we arrived
So we could buy some 7 UP before heading back

WHISKEY WILLIE

They act like you don't care, they say you really like to coast, oh no
But they don't realize what it's like to have to live with that ghost,
ah yeah
You taught me wrong from right, how to drink and how to fight,
oh no, ah yeah
Now that I am a man, I can understand
A lot of people have said you're bad
And I know at times that you made mom mad
But I have to tell you that I am real glad
And I'm always proud to call you dad
I love you Whiskey Willie
I remember on that summer day
When you packed your things and you drove away
They just don't know what it's like to have to live with that ghost,
oh no
Sometimes it takes from you all the things that you want the most,
ah yeah
Now I can match your life, I lost my mind and lost a wife, oh no,
ah yeah
Now that I am a man, I can understand
A lot of people have said you're bad
And I know at times that you made mom mad
But I have to tell you that I am real glad
And I'm always proud to call you dad
I love you Whiskey Willie
And I do, I do, I do, I do,
I do, I do, I do, I do—I

A SORT OF HOMECOMING

I liked her, but wasn't sure how much
She asked me to bake a cake and bring it to her apartment
I did, the unit was barely furnished
The living room had a couch, coffee table and ashtray
She sat next to me on the couch at a distance that indicated
She liked me, but wasn't sure how much
I asked why I brought a cake
She explained, her mother was coming home from prison
I wasn't sure what to do, so I placed her hand in mine
Exerting an amount of pressure
Indicating potential romance was momentarily tabled
The gesture was appreciated, a smile traced her mouth
Her shoulders began to sink, both of us leaned back
Melting comfortably into the couch, the day crawled by
About the time of evening when you turn on your headlights
The door knob turned, both of us stood
Her mother was home, she appeared agitated
And stared at her daughter
And then the cake, before saying
Memories have teeth that like to bite
And without instruction, both women went into another room
And shut the door, leaving me to wonder

POTHOLES & PRAYERS

Weeks after Mother's second divorce
It occurred to me she had never lived alone
So, I went to her house, not knowing
What to say, what to do
I turned on television, we sat down
Alice Cooper was lying on the ground
In a strait jacket, blood pouring from his ear
Mother looked annoyed
Stating Alice was just another soul
That would have to be added to her prayer list
Then the phone rang, Mother left the room
When she returned, her eyes were glazed
Whiskey Willie had hit a pothole
It was estimated he was doing 80
When he was thrown from his bike
Mother sat down
Neither one of us knew
What to say, what to do
But I believe we both realized
This was some kind of beginning to an end
And then I picked up the clicker
And turned to a more appropriate channel

MY GREEK CHORUS

Consistent with routine, I arrived home, halfway between sunset
and sunrise
The house was hot, I went outside, sat on the step and smoked a cig
A silent night, I puffed while thinking quiet shouldn't be mistaken
for stillness
Not in this neighborhood
My neighbor's door opened, a woman staggered out
Consistent with routine, she sat on a concrete stoop, dangled her legs
And smoked a cig while providing a narrative meant for everyone,
or nobody
The bottom of her face was swollen and bruised
I puffed and looked at her, she puffed and told me to mind my own
business
I went inside, the house was hot
The following night at work, we had extra blueberry muffins
They were huge, fist-sized, coated with sugar, I grabbed two
And a carton of milk, I arrived home, halfway between sunset and
sunrise
She was out, sitting on her concrete stoop, I hopped off my bike
Without invitation, I sat and handed her a muffin
We ate in silence and shared the milk
When we finished, she offered me a cigarette, it was menthol
I had my own, but she wanted to return a kindness
As I lit up, she told me
The best thing about miracles is that they even exist
But then she reminded me, I would probably never see one
If I stayed in this neighborhood

CASKETMAKER

After a 15-year absence, it was brought to my attention
Father was working a mile from my apartment
In a factory, building caskets, I paid a visit, unannounced
When I walked in, I saw a big man. Jackie Gleason big
Doing upholstery on a shiny white casket
I wasn't sure the guy was my father, but no one else was around
So I approached, stopped and stared
The moment he saw me, there was no wonder in his eyes
Just shame, and happiness, he knew who I was
So he bypassed an awkward reunion with an announcement
When I die, they'll bury me in this, the Cadillac of coffins
Then he closed the casket, and took me to lunch
Where he talked and watched until he realized
I wasn't going to hurt him
He looked ashamed, and happy
As he pulled a five-spot from his wallet
Sliding it across the table, extending his arm
Offering a handshake of truce
I had no idea, no idea how to respond
I had never felt less prepared
It was good to see my father

WIDE AWAKE IN BOMBAY

She stood bulletproof
Alone in a railway station
Just outside of Bombay
Like a protagonist in a foreign film
She was on a spiritual Hajj
A course lacking direction
Shuffling tiny feet with a big ego
Toward a train that sped into the unknown
Chance placed Mother in an aisle seat across from a Brahmin
Who questioned why Krishnamurti smoked cigarettes
And why his boxcar companion came to India
Mother explained with confidence
She quit a job of 25 years
Sold her house and all its possessions
Because truth wouldn't surface
While she was attached to material things
The holy man smiled, cupped her hand on the armrest
And explained with a clarity twice removed from shame
That she had attached to the detachment
And thus, the journey began

AT GOLDEN CHOW MEIN

In the middle of the dining room
Slumped over a table
A man in a security uniform
Thumbed through religious literature
A woman, bent with purpose
Stormed through the door and slalomed between tables
To grab the Watchtower magazine from his hand
She held it overhead and shook it violently
Screaming
They don't love you like I do
The security guard sat motionless
Then slid a fortune cookie wrapped in cellophane
Across the table
Before standing up
And leaving without a word

COCKTAILS WITH DISH

A woman sat alone at the bar ordering Johnny Walker Black
It was my cousin Dish, realizing each other, we smiled
I sidled up next to her and ordered a whiskey soda
Both of us grinned awkwardly, reading each other's tattoos
Both of us covered head to toe with permanent graffiti
Appropriate conversation eluded us
She mentioned something about Canadian phone carriers
I got off my stool, hugged her, then ordered another round
She asked how many times I'd been arrested
When I gave her a number, she slurred that my answer was competitive
She continued with confessions of living in the sex district
Revolving memberships in therapy and sobriety programs
Then she shot a brief glance that suggested she awaited judgment
I kissed her on the forehead and told her I loved her
She asked if I wanted to go to the strip club
Explaining the guy she lived with paid the bills
But romantically, she was into a girl, a dancer named Sprinkles
Then we sat through a patch of silence that seemed a mile long
My cousin looked content, she enjoyed this Black Sheep reunion
I asked if she was cool with having no pictures of kids on the fridge
And the thought of dying alone
Even though the bar was empty, she whispered
Not every funeral needs an audience

A PHONE CALL FROM MOTHER

The phone rang, I answered, before salutations were exchanged
Mother started the conversation by saying
That fucking Hitler, which I soon found out
Was in reference to a book I gave her called
The Boys in the Boat
When I explained I found the book inspiring
Mother interrupted to say
Before you look for beauty in art
First consider if it's attached to a grudge
The way those Nazis held their arms straight out
Hands open, facing up, or was it down
Either way, they make me sick
And then we remained silent until she said
It was going to freeze
So she needed to plug in her bird bath
The one I gave her for Christmas
And then we said we loved each other
An expression we were both getting used to

A WEDDING IN WISCONSIN

I hope Chuck liked the wedding cake I baked
Not one of my stronger efforts
But after all, he got married in a bar
326 miles from my house
By a bartender
Who received religious training
And credentials online
It was Chuck's second marriage
The bride's, too
At 3 a.m. I was halfway home and tired
The highway was empty
I was alone
To prevent sleepiness, I turned on the radio
Alice Cooper was talking about his conversion
He had taken Christ as his personal savior
As he pledged his allegiance, I remembered Mother
How she had said years ago
She was going to add him to her prayer list
I began to wonder if she actually followed through
But then I began to feel foolish when it occurred to me
Of course she did

DEALEY PLAZA

X marked the spot of assassination
It was applied with spray paint
Nobody within the municipality knew who did it
Or if it was authorized
The X had been a popular photo spot
Despite its location in a busy traffic lane
But days before the 50th anniversary
Of President Kennedy's death
Residents and retailers noted, the X had disappeared
City officials pointed out the world would be visiting soon
So it made perfect sense for Dealey Plaza
To be scraped to the brick to eliminate trip hazards
Residents and retailers didn't object
As long as the X was restored
City officials didn't like that idea
They felt the X was nothing more
Than a gruesome tourist magnet
A constant reminder of failure
Residents and retailers disagreed
And asked city officials what was worse
Failing your President, or forgetting them
The following morning the X had been restored
Nobody within the municipality knew who did it
Or if it was authorized

PIER 54

The moment I passed under the steel arch, I had second thoughts
The space was neglected and the emptiness made me feel
    uncomfortable
On the shore, at the end of a dilapidated dock was a woman, alone
She looked like Hilary Swank in *Million Dollar Baby*
I didn't want to frighten her, so I smiled passively from a distance
Before asking permission to sit down
After motioning her approval, we stared out onto the Hudson River
After sharing silence, she asked why I came
I was drunk, so honesty wasn't an issue
In a dream, I was told to visit a ghost from the Titanic
The woman nodded with understanding
And then she tossed me a grapefruit, I wasn't sure what to do
I don't like grapefruit, but I ate it and she explained
Seldom if ever, do spirits contact people because they're lonely
They just want to say goodbye before they erase their legacy
And cross over to a place where it feels natural to be forgotten
Then the lady looked at me and said
You'll never know how thankful the spirit was that you accepted the
    invitation
But the moment has passed, you're free to leave
As I stood, I became overwhelmed by feelings of intimacy
And wondered if it was appropriate to hug the woman before exiting
But then I realized I was sober, and felt awkward
So I left without saying a word

ALONE WITH MONET

After paying the suggested donation
It was as if a magnetic force pulled me to the second floor
To a space in the presence of Claude Monet's lily pads
I heard buzzing conversations in dialects I couldn't decipher
Except I knew the tone was reverent
15 minutes later the mob around me began to thin out
And I was alone in front of the painting
Now my entire body was consumed by joy, head to toe
Until a woman wearing a T-shirt indicating she may have run a 10K
In Oakland
Sidled up to me and asked
If traveling to Monet's gardens would not be the ultimate vacation
I told her I would prefer to stay in New York with the painting
Because if you visited the beautiful gardens in France
People would strike up conversations
And that would ruin the moment

OBSERVATIONS ON THE D-LINE

5:23 p.m.
Five fat boys sat apart
With no regard for posture
Slumping in their seats
Afraid to look away from their video games

5:30
Two angry women sat together
Both had greasy hair
They might have been swearing in Korean
When melons escaped their grocery bags

5:36
A woman across the aisle
Stared and called me tourist
When I asked how she knew
She mentioned I was smiling

5:38
Then she told me she was sad
But how sad she couldn't determine
Her chest kept getting in the way
Making it impossible to tell if her heart was bruised or broken

GOTHAM CITY

The marquee outside the Coliseum Bar
Advertised great food and drinks
But once inside, I noticed the tables were empty
Everybody sat at the bar
In a space that didn't require sunshine or enthusiasm
For an hour, we drank without talking
While television played the evening news
Halfway through another whiskey soda
The news anchor turned pale
As he reported Adam West, the original Batman, passed away
Everyone became slack-jawed as they journeyed through scrambled
    memories
Trying to recapture their definitive Batman moment
What I wouldn't have given to crawl inside their minds and take notes
Then a voice from the shadows asked
If the house was going to buy a round
The bartender bypassed the request
Clicked off the TV and shrugged his shoulders before asking
Who's gonna keep our city safe now

BLUE BEATS RED

In the middle of the city, on the middle of a frozen lake
We stood alone as she assembled a kite
And told me about the previous winter, about the old man from Iowa
Who set camp here to fill the sky, with a 60-foot whale
Tethered with cables, anchored by spikes
Dancing on wind for hours
She became quiet
I became cold
But comfort was soon forgotten when she announced
The red voice had returned
Whispering things she didn't want to believe
I wasn't sure what to say, I asked if I could help
She thought about it and said
The blue voice will level everything out
Because blue beats red
But sometimes I think the blue voice must be made of vapor
Because all the good things it says, end up fading away
Then she mentioned, we should go to Iowa and look for the whale kite
It wouldn't be hard to find
The old man lived in the town where Buddy Holly's plane crashed
And that town wasn't very big
Then she smiled, her kite climbed
And the sky was no longer empty

A CHAIN OF OBSERVATION

Positioned by the spice rack, in the pantry
Mother observed me watching her cat
Studying a bird, on the opposite side of the window
I commented it wasn't in the cat's best interest
To follow nature's course and get what it wanted
Mother paused, then shifted
Before explaining how it had occurred to her recently
That she'd lived with that cat
More years than both her husbands, combined
Her tone was delivered with a sense of achievement
Before returning to my comment and asking
If I was saying nature was flawed by design
Because if that was so, in fairness
The theory needed to apply to the entire food chain
Not just cats
I paused, then shifted
And told her of a time when Willie came home drunk
At four in the morning and went with me on my paper route
Where he confessed to me about bodies
Bodies the government had him eliminate
He told me killing was a tricky business
Because no matter how well you hid those bodies
They'd return the very second you close your eyes
Then the bird flew away, and the cat went downstairs
Mother turned on the television
And the matter was discussed no more

MRS. ROBINSON

I stepped into a tavern in St. Paul, where an old man gave me flak
For wearing a Yankees hat, he yelled across the bar
Hey Yankee boy, do you have any idea who Mrs. Robinson was
I didn't know where this was going, I couldn't see a trap
All eyes turned to me with anticipation, I answered . . . Anne Bancroft
The old man asked if I'd even seen the movie, I nodded yes
So he asked, why Paul Simon wrote (Then he sang)
We'd like to know a little bit about you for our files
We'd like to help you learn to help yourself
Look around you all you see are sympathetic eyes
Stroll around the grounds until you feel at home
Before I responded, he answered his question, with a question
Can't you see, this is a song about Joe and Marilyn
Paul Simon just inserted Mrs. Robinson because
He got paid a lot of money to write the soundtrack for *The Graduate*
But he got lazy and missed his deadline
Mrs. Robinson never got sent to an institution
But Marilyn Monroe did, right after divorcing DiMaggio
Joe still loved her, and wanted to remarry her, class act
If you're going to wear a Yankees hat, know this shit, ok
Then the old man made way for the barkeep
Who brought my drink while pointing out
All this could have been avoided if I'd just worn a Twins hat

VACATION PRISON TOUR

Fort Jefferson / Dry Tortugas

The Russian Supermodel complained about rough water
I listened like I cared. In hopes that eventually
I would be employed to apply her sunscreen
We sailed for hours as I explained the backstory of our destination
I bullied her with history
Fort Jefferson was built to protect the coast from invaders
16 million bricks, a moat and no drinking water on the entire island
This is where they sent Dr. Samuel Mudd
For complicity and conspiracy
In the assassination of President Lincoln
When the boat docked, and I began walking toward the fort
The Russian Supermodel stole my hand and steered me toward the
    beach
Informing me we only had three hours
And they'd be best spent in the water
When I reminded her I came to see Dr. Mudd's cell
She asked if I'd rather see these
As she removed her bikini top and waded into the ocean
Her smile offered gratitude, her words offered assurance
Sorry babe, I know boobs are your kryptonite
I promise I'll behave better, when we get to Alcatraz

MY MOTHER MAKES EFFORTS

Although she refuses to attend the Audubon Society board meetings
My mother spends Saturday mornings folding their fliers
Noting it's better to read the same accurate statement, thousands
    of times
Than listen to people make shit up as they go
My mother uses one part egg to two parts potato
When making potato salad for the priest
Recently, I saw her diluting Miracle Whip with mayonnaise
Explaining it's best to tone things down
When Father has to entertain Lutherans
Last week I called my mother on the phone
After we argued routinely, after we sat through silence
She broke the awkward moment by explaining
We'll probably never get "us" figured out
But that doesn't mean we should stop trying

THE NIGHT BEFORE
A LITTLE LEAGUE CHAMPIONSHIP

I forgot the equipment bag, I returned to the tournament site
I saw three young men, sitting on bleachers, next to the backstop
It was late, dark and quiet as I approached the coaching staff
Of the undefeated Buckeyes
The men I'd be coaching against the following day
The moon was full, shadows danced across the diamond
Making it hard to read their expressions
But after 25 years of coaching
You don't bother looking for joy or fear
It doesn't exist the night before a little league championship
All that's left is anticipation
As everyone remained silent, it became obvious
How much these guys loved their team, and each other
They wanted to stay in this moment, forever
I decided to leave, but before I did, I shook their hands
Complimenting them on a fine season
The Buckeyes head coach replied
They couldn't have asked for a better season
Regardless of the following day's outcome
I knew better and smirked
Realizing this had to be the first time
I might be pulling for my adversaries

BOB DYLAN'S SET LIST

Xcel Energy Center / St Paul MN / Oct 25 / 2017

Things Have Changed
It Ain't Me Babe
Highway 61 Revisited
Why Try To Change Me Now (Cy Coleman)
Sunny Days
Melancholy Mood (Frank Sinatra)
Honest With Me
Tryin' To Get To Heaven
Once Upon A Time (Tony Bennett)
Pay In Blood
Tangled Up In Blue
The September Of My Years (Frank Sinatra)
Early Roman Kings
Soon After Midnight
Desolation Row
Thunder On The Mountain
Autumn Leaves (Yves Montand)
Ballad Of A Thin Man
ENCORE
Blowin' In The Wind
That Lucky Old Sun (Frankie Lane)

ONCE IN A LIFETIME

After Jack Daniels, we switched to Crown & cola
Before eating walleye tacos, and returning to Jack Daniels
My fatherhood obligations were complete
I had given him Disneyland, HBO and home run power
While keeping opinions to myself, as his mother
Steered him through a college education
There is a moment when fathers no longer
Become affiliated with their son's future
If lucky, they get catalogued as a reference point
Tonight was our transition
And I wanted to go out on my own terms
So I took him to the Bob Dylan concert
The soundtrack of my life
The arena held 18,000, but only 8,000 attended
A slow-moving mass, white hair, shawls and canes
Five years prior, I saw Bob imitating his former self
But on this night, I sensed he was no longer interested
In imitating the imitator, he danced like a wizard
Crooning out ballads and covers
When the concert was over, my son called an Uber
I hopped into a cab, and sat with quiet gratitude
Until the driver dumped me out
At the end of the road

AT MASTEL'S HEALTH FOODS

All I wanted
Was to purchase multivitamins and a testosterone booster
But the woman in front of me meandered at the counter
Beginning her transaction by returning an item
To everyone's dismay, she has lost the receipt
My phone rang, I glanced, it was Mother
The woman making the purchase began describing
How menopause medicine damaged kidneys
I didn't know what that meant, but it made me wince
And put my phone back into my pocket
Seconds later, it rang again, when I picked up
Mother announced her cat was dead
And then she confessed that she felt closer to that cat
Than her husbands, children or parents
She paused, I paused, until the woman at the register
Called me to the counter, forcing me to hang up
Later that evening, when our conversation resumed
Mother apologized for confessing
She was better connected to a cat than her family
I smiled and assured her that not every situation
Needs an explanation to be understood
She paused, I paused
Both of us using silence to convey our love

BUDDY HOLLY CRASH SITE

In darkness, distance has no purpose, but Iowa does
Considering this, I left Omaha, alone, in hope of finding
A landscape painted with Norman Rockwell optimism
As fate would have it, such a place does exist
In a city called Clear Lake, where gravel roads direct you
To a place where you don't have to battle chatter
To a space in the middle of the field
That's just a bit further than the middle of nowhere
I stood there alone, ankle deep in ice and mud
But the sky was bright and the wind howled
With an angry voice I didn't understand
Staring at the monuments, I became overwhelmed
At how underwhelming they were
A flimsy tower with revolving Jell-O molds
A plaque of Buddy's guitar stood knee-high
Supported by poles cemented in Folgers coffee cans
For the longest time I thought of many things
None of which were related to this venue
But then my phone rang, and after I shut it off
The obvious became apparent
I had finally discovered America
But then my feet got cold
So I hopped back in my car
And pointed it toward St. Paul

MEXICANS IN THE PARKING LOT

After 14 hours in front of an oven, breeze feels good, beer tastes good
Both could be found outside, in the parking lot
Where a dozen bakers circled a cooler
Drinking beer quietly, starting without me
Most of them were half my age
All of them were Mexican
The youngest handed me a Modelo
I opened the can, tilted it and swallowed
Noticing the satisfaction of the crew
As they faced the breeze to receive a reward
That would only pay dividends
Until the cooler was empty

BATTING PRACTICE

Molitor and Oliva stood behind the cage
Marveling how Dozier's small body generated so much power
Pitch after pitch sailed over the left field wall
As he stepped out of the box, Max Kepler entered
A woman next to me asked, isn't he tall for a German
I didn't understand her question and considered a sarcastic response
But dark clouds rolled over and men rolled out tarps
So I walked alone through the concourse
To the bar behind left field
Where I drank Irish whiskey with the understanding
That only batting practice seemed to bring me the kind of peace
That church and lovers guarantee
When the barkeep brought another, I thought of my sister
The one I liked, the one in D.C.
For a moment I considered calling her but didn't
She was probably with her family, I'd be embarrassed if I slurred
But I smiled remembering how she once told me
Every time you're drunk, you get eight minutes of Nirvana
But don't ever try for nine, because Karma will count you greedy
And leave your ass in the ditch
When the barkeep brought another, I hoped the sun would return
But if it didn't
We'd get a doubleheader the following day

A NIGHT IN THE BRONX

After 50 years of waiting
After passing through the turnstile
My dream was finally realized
As I stood inside the house that Ruth built
She had bought the tickets
The Red Sox were in town
The two of us sat amidst the mayhem just beyond first base
Sounds, smells and tradition rattled in my mind
As I was visited by memories
Of Billy Martin
Of Reggie Jackson
Of eating peanuts with my Grandfather
During the top of the 6th
She asked what my favorite part of the game was
Overwhelmed, I responded by telling the truth
I got to sit next to the prettiest girl in Yankee Stadium

CHRISTMAS IN OMAHA

When a man becomes a certain age, he's allowed to quit church
Unless he's invited by his granddaughter
To Christmas Mass, such was my plight
In the sanctuary, I witnessed
Women wearing jeans adorned with fabricated holes
Men drinking Diet Mountain Dew
All these images were captured on a jumbotron
That covered the entire wall behind the pulpit
As the choir began singing "O Holy Night"
Everyone became merry, but I became defensive
I considered the flaws in their doctrine
As the ushers handed out candles, burning
When the choir began singing "Silent Night"
The congregation became illuminated
And it was in that light, that I saw my granddaughter
Glowing in joy
When she noticed me watching her
She placed her hand in mine
And at that very moment
A switch flipped on inside and I realized
I wanted to believe
If only for the moment

SUNDAY MORNING SIDEWALK

Walking south, I stared at the sidewalk
Possibly because I drank too much the night before
From the north came footsteps
I raised my head to see another
A guy, even bigger than me
Also staring at the sidewalk
Eyes intent, on my orthopedic clogs
Combined, we were close to 13 feet tall
And weighed well over 500 pounds
He had a thick gray beard and his fingers and nose
Had been broken, multiple times
In his right hand, he held a vanilla donut
Topped with rainbow sprinkles
I stared at his pastry, he stared at my clogs
Then we stared into one another's eyes.
At one time we might have challenged one another
You shall not pass! No, *you* shall not pass!
Looking back, I think it's safe to say
We were warriors no more
Maybe that wasn't a bad thing

ABOUT KLECKO

Klecko is a Master Bread Baker. He's spent close to four decades designing product lines across the Twin Cities. Currently he and the Russian Supermodel live in a mansion catty-corner from the home where F. Scott Fitzgerald wrote his first novel. He enjoys Nordic authors, French cooking and American League baseball.

PARIS MORNING
PUBLICATIONS

Paris Morning Publications is proud to feature the works of talented poets who peer deeply into their hearts and minds to examine the essentials of life—love, connection, justice, loss, work, beauty, fear and desire—and through the transformative power of their words on the page, make these essentials visible.

Launched in 2019, Paris Morning Publications is a boutique publishing house dedicated to producing thoughtful poetry books of the highest quality.

Visit us online at parismorningpublications.com for more information about upcoming titles.